A PARENT'S GUIDE TO MAKING EVERY CHILD A READER

A Parent's Guide to Making Every Child a Reader

Strategies for helping struggling readers over third grade

BY DR. SARAH SHABAZZ

Cover Art by Camila Câmara

ShaBazz Enterprise Publishing

© 2012 Victorville, CA – A guide to assist parents in helping children achieve reading success.
© 2022 Victorville, CA (2nd Edition)

Acknowledgments

Special thanks to Denise Catherwood for her editing skills and beneficial suggestions and to my son, Akhir, for his technology expertise and for helping me just for asking. To the principal(s) at my school I thank you for encouraging and supporting me to get published. Thank you to my family and friends for having the faith in me and for encouraging me to update the book. I am grateful to you all for listening to me for hours on end about my reading experiences and discoveries. Some of you have heard these stories many times and never get tired of listening to me tell you about it one more time. Thank you to my 11 children and uncountable students that gave me the personal experiences to share.

Contents

chapter	
Acknowledgments	v
	vii

1	Introduction	1
2	An Interesting Analogy Regarding the Achievement Gap	3
3	Reading and Personal Background	6
4	Older Struggling Readers	10
5	"Oh Lord, This Child Can't Read"	12
6	History Repeats Itself	14
7	Sight Words	20
8	Valuing Vocabulary	22
9	Flowing with Fluency	26
10	Phonemic Awareness	28
11	The Reality of Reading	29
12	Sustained Silent Reading	30
13	Selecting Reading Material	32
14	Teaching Older Readers New Tricks	34
15	Adults Can Learn to Read	37

16	Activities to Increase Reading Skills of Older Readers	41
17	Technology in Reading	44
18	Activities and Strategies that Work	48
19	Sample Study	49
20	Reading is Developmental	61
21	Common Core	63
22	Reading and Distance Learning	65
23	Ortin Gillingham	67
24	Strategies and Activities	69

About the Author   71
More Books by Dr. ShaBazz   73

Copyright © 2022 by By Dr. Sarah ShaBazz

All rights reserved. No part of this book may be reproduced in any manner whatsoever without written permission except in the case of brief quotations embodied in critical articles and reviews.

First Printing, 2012

Chapter 1

Introduction

    I chose to focus on reading because reading is the foundation of education. As the slogan states, "Reading is Fundamental." My original interest was in the achievement gap, but I narrowed it down to reading because I feel that that is a major component of the problem with the achievement gap. The achievement gap is the difference in the scores of two groups, such as low income and high income students or white students and students of color. I researched three theorists and I discovered that each had their own theories of reading and education based on their personal experience. Les Vygotsky was of the belief that students struggling with reading needed more time in a small setting with an adult or competent reader. His Zone of Proximal Development (ZPD) theory states that a child can read independently with comprehension in his ZPD level. When a child reads with an adult, he reads at a higher level. The adult provides assistance and scaffolds the child to the next level. Children should be encouraged to read within their ZPD. This is best accomplished when children choose something of interest on his/her reading level, such as children magazines or special interest books.

W.E.B. Dubois had a childhood that was rich with reading. His mother's bookshelves held all the classics. In contrast, Booker T. Washington was nearly an adult when he learned to read. He was born during slavery when black people were not allowed to read, and then later had to help with farm work rather than attend school when the opportunity became available. He attended night school to learn to read, then later opened night classes to other adults in need of the skill.

Chapter 2

An Interesting Analogy Regarding the Achievement Gap

It is well known that black slaves were not allowed to learn to read or write. I recently overheard a conversation between two young African American women who had attended historically black colleges. One of the young women gave an interesting analogy about why many black people continue to struggle academically. She explained it like this. There are two people running a race, in which one is skilled and the other one is unprepared. The first person, representing the white race, is allowed a three-and-a-half day (or 365 years) head start. The second person, representing the black race, is held down and not allowed to run.

After the three and a half days have lapsed, the second runner is released and allowed to begin running. The second runner is teased, taunted, and called discouraging names. He is told that he has just as much opportunity to run as the first runner and that there is no excuse for his lack of ability to catch up. The fact that three and a half days have passed and that many hours have come and gone is not taken into consideration. This analogy of a race is used to represent the black slave not being allowed to read until after emancipation. Even today, many black people are still lagging academically. As the conversation continued, I heard one of the young ladies explain further. The young lady explained that black people are told that they should be just as smart as white people because they have the same opportunities. (After all, some black people have caught up and even passed white people, so what is wrong with the others?) It is not impossible for a runner to catch up to someone that began running three and a half days ahead of him, if he/she were equally trained to do so. Those who have caught up and exceeded academically are exceptional scholars who have been taught skills that helped them catch up and even surpass the expectations of the very ones who discouraged them.

Many runners would lose interest in trying to catch up with someone so far ahead. They would feel that there is no use. Some would do the best they could, but would not expect to catch up.

I think this applies in part to the achievement gap. There were generations of people who never learned to read. For many there was no interest and no need. They were able to survive without that skill and did not pressure their offspring to master reading either. Others embraced the opportunity and took full advantage. Some learned only because they were forced to do it once school became a requirement. Is this really the underlying *cause* of the achievement gap?

As explained above, the achievement gap is the difference in the academic progress of white students compared to the progress of black students. There is a difference (gap) in the scores received by each group of students. When comparing this to the previously explained competitive race scenario, it is not difficult to see how this may very well have contributed to the nationwide ever-increasing achievement gap.

Chapter 3

Reading and Personal Background

I found that the aforementioned theorists' own personal experience seriously shaped their individual beliefs. Here I include my own personal experiences with reading as it directly relates to some of the problems experienced by struggling readers in grades four to six. Many students in this age group missed basic concepts, either due to learning or reading disabilities or lack of exposure. Learning or reading disabilities would require that a student have more time on tasks and more direct instruction in a small group setting. Lack of exposure is usually the result of frequent absences, changing schools often or just never being taught the concepts.

My grandmother read nursery rhymes to me daily. I had memorized all of them by the time I began attending school in Louisiana at the age of five. I was already able to write and recite my alphabet and I could spell and write my first and last name. I learned to read from repetition and memorization.

The teacher would say, and I would repeat, "See Susan run, Susan can run and run." Our first soft-cover reader was *My Little Red Story Book*. Once that book had been mastered, we read *My Little Blue Story Book* and *My Little Green Story Book*. They were soft-cover books. The characters in the books were, Susan, Betty, Tom, Mother, Father, the dog Flip and the cat Frisky.

Once those three books were mastered, we moved on the hardcover book, *The Big White House*. I was one of the best readers in the class and was well into the hardcover book by the end of first grade. The teacher told my grandmother I was reading from the second grade book. Over the summer I moved to California. The following fall I attended second grade at a small private school. The second grade reader was the same book I had in first grade. I read very well until I got to the part I had not memorized yet. At that point I began to struggle. I did not understand the concept of sounding out words. I had not learned phonics and did not know or understand that each letter had a sound. It was all foreign to me. I had learned to read from repetition and memorization. Once I learned a word I always knew it. I had no clue how to sound a word out. My teacher became frustrated with me. She could not understand why suddenly I could no longer read.

I remember one incident where I was standing in class reading aloud and came upon a word I didn't know. I read, "The, the, the...." I was hoping she would tell me the word. Instead she replied, "If you say *the* one more time, I don't know what I'm going to do to you." I didn't know what she was going to do to me either, but it didn't sound good. After that, I began to read ahead to learn my part before my turn came. I listened to the other students read and remembered the words. I wrote words down and asked about them at home. I was very quiet and I did not talk. I didn't want the other students or the teacher to know that I had trouble reading unknown words.

There was a little girl in my second grade class that was not a good reader at all. In fact, it would be fair to say she was the lowest reader in the class. In the middle of the school year she was in a car accident that put her in the hospital for a while. She missed three months of school, and when she returned she was the best reader in the class. She had been given a private tutor while she was out of school. The tutor helped her to develop her reading skills and she read with perfect diction and fluency. The results of one-on-one tutoring were evident in this case.

As I progressed in school, comprehension became a problem for me; I would have to read things over again and again in order to understand what I was reading. Sometimes I skipped the words I didn't know, which hindered my comprehension even more. Vocabulary didn't come easy for me because I didn't know how to pronounce the words. One thing that helped was the books that came with records my mother purchased for me. She bought all the classic children stories, such as *The Three Little Pigs, The Three Bears, Hansel and Gretel* and *The Ugly Duckling*. I would listen to the records and follow along in the book. This was a tremendous boost to my reading vocabulary. I never learned phonics so I had to continue memorizing words to add to my reading vocabulary.

Even after I had completed college and had a teaching credential, I didn't have the mastery of phonics. I would pre-read the lessons for my ninth grade English students to make sure I knew the words before I attempted to teach. The instructional assistant that was assigned to me had majored in English in college and had a very good vocabulary. I would approach her with any questions I had regarding the proper way to pronounce a word. I usually made the case for my mispronunciation due to how we said it in Louisiana. Some words such, as "genre," I could not attempt to pronounce correctly. I knew what it meant, but had never heard it pronounced.

My story contains all the components of struggling readers in today's classroom: silent students who cover up their reading deficits, difficulty with comprehension and vocabulary, the effectiveness of tutoring, repeated readings, and listening to recorded books. Several strategies including but not limited to story mapping, best practices for staff development, and student success skills for older readers are other important elements for closing the achievement gap by assisting struggling readers.

Chapter 4

Older Struggling Readers

The reason I am focusing on the older struggling reader is because they get less attention and assistance. Instruction for older students does not include improving reading skills, but rather using the skills that have already been acquired. Just yesterday while browsing through a magazine at the dentist's office I read that 57% of fourth grade African American males are functionally illiterate, which means they can do just enough to get by. This is not acceptable. I have read many articles about older struggling readers and found that the results were the same. Students lack rich vocabularies, which affect comprehension. When reading at an independent level, vocabulary is not improved because that level is far below the student's grade level. When reading grade level material, students struggle to comprehend because they are not familiar with the words they read and have no background knowledge of the content.

Many schools are not providing the extra time and attention needed on a broad scale. Yet, the studies which have been done and the pilot programs that have been put into place prove time and time again that this is a problem that *can* be fixed. The National Reading Panel (2000) clearly explains all the component of reading: phonemic awareness, phonics, decoding, vocabulary, fluency and comprehension. The lower grades are taught phonemic awareness, phonics and decoding. Many older students have mastered these concepts, but are stifled in their reading progress because of lack of skills in the other areas such as vocabulary and comprehension.

Chapter 5

"Oh Lord, This Child Can't Read"

My first encounter with an older nonreader occurred when I was in the sixth grade attending a small private school in Los Angeles, California. It was the first day back to school and the class had been assigned the usual essay, "My Summer Vacation." We should have had it prepared when we came on the first day, because we had to write it every fall upon our return to school. We were all busy writing when I heard the teacher say, "Why aren't you writing? You haven't started yet." The student replied in a whisper, "I don't know what to write." She was encouraged to think about what she had done this summer and get started. The teacher became distracted with the other students and soon it was recess time. All the students had been dismissed for recess. I was lagging behind, trying to get something from my lunch pail, when I heard the teacher talking to the student regarding her lack of progress. The teacher said, "You didn't even write your name." Tears began to stream from the student's eyes and I heard the teacher say, "Oh Lord, this child can't read." Even though I was a child myself, I shared the devastation of the moment. It had a lasting and profound effect on me.

This was a fifth/sixth grade combination class. There were a total of 22 students.

Over the course of the year, the student made great strides. She was held back in the fifth grade for the next year, but ended up graduating with the sixth grade class. She had learned to read and write and could perform on grade level. This illustrates that with time and direct instruction, older students can catch up to grade-level peers. I was later told by the student's sixth grade teacher the student went on to complete high school, attend a Jr. College, and become employed. She then sent her children to the same private school.

Chapter 6

History Repeats Itself

I had a tear-jerking moment of my own thirty years later. I was the resource teacher for fourth through sixth grade. A boy was sent to me for extra help. The teacher had explained that he could not read. I began testing him with the alphabet and he knew all of the letters. Next, I had him read from the kindergarten sight-word list. He could not read *at*, or *the*, but he knew *a*. I immediately thought back on the incident which had occurred with my sixth grade teacher as I fought to hold back the tears. We worked on his reading several hours a day, and just as he really began to read, he moved. Later I encountered a fourth grade student with no phonemic awareness. He did not know or understand that each letter had a sound. He had memorized many words, but could not decode. If he came across a word he didn't know, he would just make up a word and keep reading. Sometimes he would even make up full sentences or complete paragraphs. He would read with a serious look on his face at a steady pace, as if he was reading the correct words.

I had to teach him new words by memorization and repetition, the same way I had learned myself. I used the Edmark program, which uses repetition and memorization. The student added new words to his repertoire at each session. Once he learned a word, he knew it.

So I have to disagree wholeheartedly that students not reading by the end of third grade will never catch up. Here's why. I have two other cases where African American females were not reading by the end of third grade. One learned to read in a small group setting while in the sixth grade. She states she really wanted to know how to read. She remained quiet in her regular classroom and did not talk much. Once she began being pulled out into the resource room, she made every effort to improve her reading. She volunteered to read out loud in the smaller setting. She did not feel threatened, because none of the students in the room had good reading skills. They were all there for the same purpose. By the end of sixth grade, the student was reading on grade level and even made honor roll. She went on to complete high school, attended college on an academic scholarship, graduated with honors (Magna Cum Laude), went to law school, passed the California Bar exam and became an attorney.

A second case is an African American woman who said she really did not begin reading until her sophomore year in high school. She stated that there were many reading assignments. She had to read classic novels such as *The Catcher in the Rye*. During that time she also read books from the *Goosebumps* series and other chapter-book series independently. She said that she had to read slowly and reread sentences until the content made sense, and that she used context clues to help her with comprehension. The young woman went on to graduate high school and went on to college where she obtained a bachelor's degree.

In 2010, I have worked with a student who went from a pre-primer level in reading to a strong fifth grade reading level. This was a two-year process, during which the student gained six years of reading skills. The second week of school it was brought to my attention by a classroom teacher that a student was reading on pre-primer level. The teacher told me that the parent wrote her a note and stated the student could not read, and please do not ask her to read in front of the class and embarrass her. When the student was tested via computer along with the other students in the class, she indeed scored pre-primer.

I began working with this student immediately. She made every excuse known to man to get out of my classroom. One day she would complain about her stomach and the next day she would have a headache. I eventually told her that she was not leaving the room unless she was dead. So she might as well get ready to read. We used books on tape, in addition to learning the phonics rules. I provided the web address for www.starfall.com to her mother and explained that she should use it as home as much as possible. By the end of fifth grade, the student was reading at a solid third grade level. At the beginning of sixth grade, she was able to read at a mid-third grade level. Her mother told me that she continued to read throughout the summer. She then read 32 words per minute of sixth grade text—her actual grade.

The student received specialized, direct instructions for thirty minutes a day, four times a week. Her progress was monitored every other week. She read a sixth-grade level passage for one minute. By the end of the year, she was consistently reading over 100 words per minute on a sixth grade level. The words she read per minute varied from 107 to 121, but she was able to consistently read over 100 words per minute. We determined her level was fifth grade at the end of the year because she was able to read fifth grade level passages with ease and answer comprehension questions with 90% accuracy.

Although most of the scenarios I have described involve females learning to read after third grade I have no doubt that it would work the same way for either gender. I think that society and educational professionals should get away from the way of thinking that a child is doomed for life if they cannot read after third grade. It is simply not true. The reason this was so widely accepted is because students are not taught to read after third grade and no instruction is provided to help them improve their reading. This improved after the implementation of the Common Core State Standards.

When I wrote the first edition of this book, I stated, "The federal No Child Left Behind program currently in place needs to be realigned to include daily reading interventions for students above third grade who are reading below grade level". I felt that emphasis should be placed on learning to read until the skill is mastered. Once reading is mastered, the other core curriculum subjects can be undertaken. The ability to read will assist in making progress in all other subjects. Students should read core curriculum material at their functioning reading level and not be forced to read grade level text that is far beyond their ability. This way they can acquire knowledge in the grade level standards and be exposed to needed information while reading, without becoming frustrated.

Many school districts do not feel like they have the time to contribute to school-wide reading programs. They feel there is too much ground to be covered to spend ninety minutes a day on reading only. I feel that every child can be and should be a reader. We need support from the federal government to fully support every child to become a reader. Funding and professional development should be provided to insure that all students receive adequate and sufficient time to improve their reading skills in any grade as long as they are in need of the support.

Side Bar: There has been some improvement in this area, at least in the school district where I teach. All teachers have been trained in Guided Reading and provided with materials for teaching reading. Additionally, free before and after school tutoring also became available for any and all students needed extra reading help.

Every child in the elementary school where I teach was assessed three times a year to determine their Zone of Proximal Development (ZPD). This is the level where students can read independently with comprehension. The first test is done within the first two weeks of school in the fall. The second test is in November to determine growth, and the final test is done in May again to measure growth. The books in the library are coded with colored dots to indicate the level of the book. Students are taught to select books within their ZPD. Once the book is read by the student, they take a quiz on the computer. The computer records all tests taken by the student. A score of 85% or better is required by the school. The computer allows students to still pass the quiz with a score as low as 60%, but any score lower than 85% is not considered proficient.

There are also school-wide incentive programs in place. One program is Fun Friday, where the students get to have fun treats and activities after lunch on Friday if they meet their weekly goal, which is achieved by making a set amount of points. There is also the Star Reader award, which is awarded to students making thirty points within a trimester with 85% comprehension or higher. There is an awards ceremony where T-shirts and certificates are given to the students.

Students begin using the Accelerated Reader program in first grade. In the beginning the books are read to the students, and then later read with the students. By the end of first grade the students are reading the books independently.

Most picture books are only worth half a point. Chapter books are worth one point. Very large chapter books on higher grade levels, such as the *Harry Potter* series, can be worth as much thirty points.

The reason I chose to research Les Vygotsky as a theorist on reading is because I use his theories daily to improve students' reading. The majority of the students that I work with that have reading deficits are African American males. I studied both Booker T. Washington and W.E.B. Dubois because they too are African American males. I felt their input would be favorable to the students involved.

Of the many articles I read, the one that I found the most intriguing regarded the Student Success Skills study. In this study, students were taught success skills that included setting goals, progress monitoring, nutrition and exercise. The gap was closed with the participants in this study. There was no emphasis placed on the actual teaching of reading or math. The students were taught how to achieve success by having high expectations of themselves and taking care of their body as well as their mind. They were given a can-do attitude. There was an increase in self-worth, self esteem, and personal pride.

Chapter 7

Sight Words

It is very important to get your child to know and recognize sight words with automaticity. That means they know the word when they see it without hesitation, like they would know their own name. Explain to your child that the sight words have to be recognized at sight (as soon as they see them). Explain that sight words cannot be sounded out because most of them do not follow the rules, and that is why they are sight words. There are several sight words lists. You can easily find one by using Google. The most popular sight word lists are the Fry sight word list or the Dolch sight word list. All the lists pretty much have the same words, but they are presented in a different order. Your child's school may have grade level sight word lists. If this is the case begin with the kindergarten sight word list. Once one list is mastered, move on to the next list. To get started, make two copies of the list. One is for the child to read from and one is for you to follow along and mark the words the child misses. Once you have identified the words that your child does not know, make flashcards. Play a game where if the child gets the word right they get the card, and if they miss the word you keep the card. After all the cards have been read, have the child count the number of cards he/she has to determine who wins the game. Review the missed words with the child. Teach them the words they missed and then play the game until the child can win all the cards. There is a free website, www.spellingcity.com, where you can put some words in for the child to learn to spell. This will be helpful because they will learn to spell the words so that they can use them in their writing.

Note: Do not allow the child to put the words in themselves, to avoid them from practicing and learning the words incorrectly.

Chapter 8

Valuing Vocabulary

Vocabulary seems to be a major component of lack of comprehension in older struggling readers. The Matthew Effect explains that good readers get better and poor readers get worse. Good readers improve their vocabulary as they read more; they gain more vocabulary. Poor readers do not read on grade level and have to read lower level books, which does not increase their vocabulary. Many students have very good decoding skills and can decode and sound out any word, but once the word is read they do not know what the word means so the comprehension is hindered.

Vocabulary was a major struggle for me. While I was still very young I decided I didn't want a large vocabulary and I would use simple words that everyone could understand. As I got older I had difficulty understanding what people meant when they spoke. Often times I would have to write the word down and look it up when I got home in order to understand what had been said to me. When I was a freshman in college, I was taking a bowling class. Every ball I threw was a gutter ball, without fail. I scored perfectly on the written test, but had a major problem getting the ball down the lane. One day halfway through the semester the teacher said, "Well at least you're consistent." I smiled and nodded, not knowing what consistent meant. This was before the time of Google and smart phones, so I went home and looked "consistent" up in the dictionary. Another time I was having a conversation with a gentleman and in the course of the conversation I mentioned I had seven children. He made the comment, "You are very prolific." I had no idea what he meant. Again I had to resort to my dictionary, only to find it meant fertile. These are only two examples of the many times I was not able to use context clues to determine the meaning of unknown words.

I read a study that was done on college campuses where college students were asked if they believed in women's suffrage. The study revealed that the majority of the students answered no, not knowing that suffrage was the right to vote. They assumed it meant to suffer. I had an interesting conversation with a man who took great pride in his extensive vocabulary. He would literally laugh at his ability to insult people without them knowing it. His favorite thing to do was tell people that they were the most, crass person he had ever met, while smiling at them—and many people had no idea he was calling them stupid. It is important to teach our students the meaning of words and encourage them to build their vocabularies.

Synonyms are a great method of teaching vocabulary. Students can keep a journal or personal thesaurus to write down larger words with the same meaning as smaller words. When reading with an adult, children should ask questions about unknown vocabulary in order to build their reading vocabulary. Adults need to volunteer examples of what words mean in order give meaning to the students.

I encourage parents to substitute larger words for smaller known words. For example, when ordering at a restaurant, ask the child which beverage he/she would prefer rather than what drink he/she wants. Refer to the child's sister and brothers as siblings and the dog as a canine. Call your husband or wife your spouse and refer to money as currency. These simple word substitutions will increase the child's reading vocabulary and they will not be stumped by the meaning of words they come across while reading. Also, the more they read and are able to read on grade level, the more their vocabulary will increase. Students who score well on the SAT are usually avid readers and have read the classic literature that exposes them to an abundance of vocabulary words.

Let me share a couple of interesting stories. Our family relocated to a new city where we rented until we purchased our home. Shortly after our family moved in, my daughter told me that the landlord had come by and told her to let us know that he'd left a newspaper in the backyard. The message seemed strange, but we didn't think anything of it. Soon after we got home the landlord came back by the house and explained that he had lost an article in the backyard and wanted to know if we would assist him in locating it. The "article" was his wedding ring. The only article my daughter was familiar with was a newspaper article, and therefore she assumed he was looking for a newspaper. That day my daughter learned that an article was another name for an item or a thing.

Once when we were driving on our way to school, my daughter questioned the smoke in the distance. She wanted to know if something was on fire. My son said, "No that is from the plant." My daughter questioned, "What is it, a burning bush or something?" I laughed as I explained to her plant was another name for factory. It is very important that children understand that some words have more than one meaning and they should be familiar with them.

It is also important to make sure that your children know the correct words for things. Sometimes they may only be accustomed to using the slang word and not know that actual meaning of a word. Here is an example. My youngest son was about five years old when he had dressed himself one morning. When I saw him I told him, "Those pants are tight" (meaning too small). He smiled and with a big grin on his face and replied, "Yes, my pants are tight", you like them? I had to explain to him that tight means too small or too little and he needed to change his pants. He had learned the word tight from him teenage brothers. They used it to mean cool or fly (nice).

Comprehension is another major deficit for older struggling readers. Sometimes they read, but do not understand. Vocabulary is sometimes the cause, but sometimes the student spends so much time trying to decode the words that they cannot concentrate on what they are reading. So much time and effort is put into the reading itself that no meaning is obtained. The child just reads and does not listen to what is being read or think about the content. In addition, sometimes the students lack prior knowledge of the concept being read and cannot make a personal connection to it. Several strategies help improve comprehension: (1) repeated reading; (2) listening to someone else read the same passage, and this can be done by a person or a recording; (3) story maps are a great method of building comprehension, because they help children to see the whole picture by organizing thoughts and concepts graphically.

Chapter 9

Flowing with Fluency

Fluency is reading with a steady pace using the correct tone, diction and rhythm. Someone reading with fluency does not sound choppy, as if they are calling out words. For struggling readers, modeling is a good method of teaching fluency. The Read Naturally program uses recorded nonfiction passages. The student listens to the passage three times prior to practicing the passage on his/her own. The combination of the repeated reading and the modeled recording helps improve the reader's fluency. Comprehension also improves with fluency. Once the student is no longer struggling to read the words and can read them fluently, they can listen to themselves read and focus on what is being read.

Comprehension, fluency and vocabulary are the three major deficits of older struggling readers. However, there are instances where there is no phonemic awareness or no knowledge of phonics, times when an older child can not read at all. Theses cases are not the norm. They should be treated on an individual basis. Older students with these deficits need to start from the beginning and work up. It is a very time-consuming task, but is needed to get the student to become a confident reader.

Chapter 10

Phonemic Awareness

Phonemic awareness is something that can be done in the dark or with the eyes closed. You do not need to see to perform phonemic awareness tasks. They consist of things such as beginning word sounds, ending words sounds, middle vowel sounds, and rhyming words. Phonics, on the other hand, is the knowledge that each written letter is associated with a sound. To know phonics is to know that each of the vowels has both a long and short sound, the vowel combination, diphthongs and digraphs. It is basically knowing all the necessary pieces to the reading code in order to decode words. Decoding is the next step after phonics. It is the ability to use phonics to sound out or decode unknown words.

It has been determined that older struggling readers can become confident readers with extra help and time dedicated to improving reading skills. Why then is there not ample classroom time placed on this growing deficit? The ability to read can make a great impact on one's potential quality of life.

Chapter 11

The Reality of Reading

There was a time when reading did not reap benefits for everyday life. Life could be lived without even coming in contact with the written word. Those days are long gone. Reading is required in order to lead a successful life. Jobs are competitive and the person with the better skills is more likely to get the job. Tests are required for employment and driver's licenses. In addition to reading, written skills are also needed to complete applications for renting or buying a home, purchasing a car, or registering for school. Once employed, there are the rules and regulations of the handbook to be read, job postings, various directions and instructions, as well as memos.

Reading is a fact of life. It never goes away. Reading occurs in all parts of everyday life. It is not possible to avoid reading in the course of a day. Street signs, billboards, advertisements, and business names are everywhere.

Chapter 12

Sustained Silent Reading

Some schools participate in programs such as Sustained Silent Reading (SSR) or Drop Everything and Read (DEAR). These programs work very well with students that are competent readers. The more they read, the better they get at reading and the more they build their vocabularies. However, struggling readers do not benefit from sustained silent reading. Let me repeat that: Struggling readers *do not benefit* from sustained silent reading. Struggling readers need guidance and support. They need to read with adults or peer-age competent readers. They need to have reading modeled for them. When a struggling reader reads without support, they skip over words they do not know. Skipping words makes it very difficult to comprehend what is being read. Many times, struggling readers don't really read. They hold the book (sometimes) and turn the pages (sometimes), but they are not reading what they hold in front of them.

I had a conversation some years ago with a new high school principal. He was telling me about this new program that had proven effective in a pilot study. He said that they had piloted the program for a year and all students had made growth in reading. I questioned him on the reading ability of the students prior to being selected for the pilot. I was told that all the students were in Advanced Placement (AP) classes. I explained to the principal that his results were not valid for improving the reading of students that need to improve. I told him that students that read well only get better with practice. He disagreed with me and said the results were valid and the program would work. The following fall, his school implemented a program where student had fifty minutes of silent reading while a teacher sat in a desk at the front of the room and did not provide any reading instructions. The principal went in each week to offer incentives to whichever student

made the most progress. No progress was made, and the following semester the class was cancelled. The teacher was not trained to teach reading to high school students and did not know how to provide reading instructions to them. This was a regular education class and it was not taught by a teacher who would have had the training to teach reading, such as a reading specialist.

If you are going to give your child a book to read alone, make sure it is something that you have already read and are familiar with. This way you can question him/her on the content of the text. Ask questions to make sure the child understand what he/she is reading. Choose and point to larger words in the book to determine if the child can read and understand the words that are in the text.

Chapter 13

Selecting Reading Material

How do you know what to select for your child to read? First, it is a good idea to make sure it is within the child's ability range. The Zone of Proximal Development (ZPD) is a level at which a child can read independently without frustration. It is alright to choose books that are above the child's independent level if it is something you will be reading together. This way you can provide the needed support and assist the child with reading unfamiliar words. One method of determining if a book is too difficult is to have the child place an open hand on the page of a book. Ask the child to read each word that appears directly above each finger. These will be random words (due to the length of the fingers). If the child can read four of the five words without difficulty, the book is within his/her independent range. If the child struggles with the words, the book is too difficult. If the child reads all the words with ease, turn the page and try again. Children can learn from books that are easy to read especially if the genre is nonfiction, or real-life stories.

The child will gain a better understanding of the information if they can read it easily.

Chapter 14

Teaching Older Readers New Tricks

The PIAT (Putting it All Together) Method, which I developed, is geared toward the reading success of older readers that missed the initial interventions provided. It is intended to be taught in a small setting, and should take no longer than one school year. Part of the reason this program was developed was to accelerate progress. There are many programs such as Jane Fell Green's Language! program, which has all the components of improving reading in older students, but is a lengthy process that takes several years to complete.

Note: Language! Live is new version which is now half online and half classroom workbooks. There are four books for $7^{th} - 12^{th}$ grades.

Part of the reason for acceleration is because the transit and mobility rates are increasing and students need to get caught up as quickly as possible. Another reason for the fast track is because students need to be at or above grade level to receive the maximum benefit of the concepts being taught in class.

The quicker grade level proficiency can be attained, the more beneficial it will be for the student.

The new Response to Intervention (RtI) process covers this aspect of teaching and learning reading. All students that are below grade level are identified by the teacher. The classroom teacher provides additional help to the students using research-based programs. If the student responds, success is achieved. If the student does not respond, they are moved to the next level to provide more direct instruction in a smaller setting. This usually works, but if it does not, the last and final level is to provide more intense instruction in even a smaller setting and help students with learning disabilities or deficits in whatever way works best for the student. Very few students will get to this level of instruction. It is not required for students unless there is a cognitive problem or a severe deficit.

Side Bar: RTI has now been replace with MTSS (Multi- Tier system of Support) New name same concept.

In order to develop best practices for classroom teachers to use on a wide scale,

a method needs to be set in place to support teachers with consideration of all the tasks their job includes. At this time I am seeking the best method of delivering fast, effective intervention in the small group setting, provided by the resource teacher. This limits the amount of students that can receive extra help at one time because group size has to remain small for the intervention to be successful.

Schools should provide workshops for the parents of struggling readers periodically. The workshops should be set in place as a support system. If the workshops are offered two or three times a year, a parent can have a greater opportunity of attending the one most suitable to their schedule. This will also allow parents to attend the workshop more than once to reinforce the strategies that best train parents how to help their children.

There should also be a widespread campaign to train reading tutors to assist struggling readers. There should be a federally funded program to train parent volunteers, college and high school students, retired people and anyone else interested in making every child a reader. But the clock is winding down. NCLB has set the year 2014 as the year all children should be performing at grade level. The first step is to get them reading. This can be accomplished, but the system in place has to make some social changes and embrace a new support system to provide the needed help to struggling readers.

Side Bar: NCLB (No Child Left Behind) was replaced by Common Core State Standards.

Chapter 15

Adults Can Learn to Read

I mentioned earlier that Booker T. Washington learned to read as an adult. He then encouraged and taught other adults to read. These adults learned to read because they wanted to know how to read. They received adequate instructions to assist them in completing the task. This was a growing trend, because slaves had not been allowed to learn to read. Once slavery was over, the opportunity to read was granted. Many former slaves took advantage of it. Reading made life easier and more satisfying because they were able to gain higher education and employment opportunities.

In 1987, a television movie called *Bluffing It*, starring Dennis Weaver, came out. Dennis Weaver played a blue-collar worker who had never learned to read, but had fooled everyone in his life (including his own family) into thinking that he could. The truth eventually came out after he was promoted to foreman at work, and had to learn how to use a computer. He almost caused the death of someone on a highway because he could not read a sign. At the end of the movie, he was learning how to read. It makes you wonder how many people out there are really "bluffing it."

More recently and in real life, the 2004 American Idol, Fantasia Barrino, went public with her own story of bluffing it. She had already won the American Idol title and had also already written a book of her memoirs (in which she did not reveal her secret) when she came forth with the truth. She said she revealed her secret to the world in the hopes that it would help other young women in the same situation and encourage them to seek help. Fantasia explained that she wanted to change her limiting condition and had paid a private tutor to assist her in improving her reading skills. I do not know Fantasia and am only stating what I have read. I do not know the level of Fantasia's reading prior to seeking help or her level after she had received instructions. I do know that I would have been able to provide the needed instructions to make Fantasia a competent reader.

The reason I know this is because I have provided private tutoring myself to an adult who had been bluffing it throughout his life. This man was in his mid thirties and had a wife and children. Much like the Dennis Weaver character in the movie, he had a blue -collar job which he had been working for many years. He had been asked to promote up to foreman, but declined because he was aware that he would have to take a test and would also have to write reports once he took the position. My initial assessment of the student included a writing assignment. I asked him to write one page on any topic he desired. The written sample was much like that of a first grader, with many spelling errors and the usage of creative spelling. I use the phrase "creative" rather than phonemic because the spelling was random, not consistent, and did not follow any phonemic rules.

We began our instruction by reviewing the alphabet sounds. He knew them without a problem when they were isolated. However, blends and vowel combinations were a different story. He did not know the rules or sounds for them. One thing about this student was I rarely had to tell him the same thing more than once. Once I explained a rule, he made it his own and remember it for future uses. Also, due to his age and experience, he had incredible background knowledge and great comprehension. Many times he would decode an unfamiliar word and automatically know the meaning. I know this because I would often ask, "Do you know what that means?"

Once we reviewed the alphabet sounds we began working on the vowels with short and long vowel rules and then diphthongs (vowel combinations) and digraphs (consonant blends). After that we worked on prefixes, suffixes, and root words. This assisted the student in learning to break down larger words with multi-syllables. Each week we reviewed the previously learned words. We then read a passage, practiced spelling and writing, had a spelling test, and wrote a paragraph. In less than six months I felt the student was a competent reader. I told him that he read as well as I did. He wanted to continue his instructions indefinitely, but I had other commitments and I felt he had all he needed to be successful. I provided him with all the tools he needed to be a competent reader. He had filled in all the holes and deficits. He didn't need me anymore, and I didn't think it was healthy for him to rely on me.

Just a few weeks ago I was in a meeting with a parent discussing his daughter's difficulty with reading. The father explained that he himself hadn't learned to read until he was in the fifth grade. I inquired about his experience and he explained that he had a teacher who took interest in him once it was discovered that he was a non-reader. The teacher told him that he was a smart kid and could learn to read if he wanted to. He spent extra time after school practicing his reading. He said the teacher showed him that it was not hard. The father proudly stated that, "Now I read as well as anyone else."

Chapter 16

Activities to Increase Reading Skills of Older Readers

Read to your child. Yes, even older children enjoy being read to. I remember a college level class I took where the teacher began each lesson by reading a children's book to the class. Even as adults, the gesture was well received. If your child does not want to hear classic children's books, read something else. Read a chapter book of interest to the student by reading a little each day. Read the biographies of famous people and discuss their contributions.

Read with your child. You can take turns reading alternate pages, or you can read a lot and have the child read a little. Show interest in the books your child selects. Ask them what they think will happen next. Tie what you read to real life situations. Say things like, "Remember when_____ happened? It is almost the same as the book!" Set aside times when you will read. I remember my four daughters and I read *Little Women* together one weekend when I was braiding their hair. We passed the book around and took turns. Afterwards, we watched two versions of the movie and had a discussion to compare and contrast the book and two different movies.

Have your child read the recipe while you cook. Have them read off the grocery list as you shop. Have them read the printed directions from Google or Yahoo maps (although it might be a good idea to know where you are going in advance). Have your child read and respond to incoming text messages for you when are busy and can't do it yourself. Sometimes it is a good idea to mute the television and use the closed captions where the writing appears on the screen. You and the child can take turns reading the captions.

Have your child read a familiar book to a younger sibling or relative. The younger child will beam with excitement and think the older child is the smartest person alive. Also have your child read a familiar book to an elder person; this can be a relative, a friend or just a neighbor. The best way to improve reading is by reading.

Research shows that multiple readings (reading the same thing more than once) increases both fluency and comprehension. Have your child read the same thing several times. In the beginning they might protest, saying that they already read it. Explain to your child that they listen to the same music on their iPod over and over, and that they look at the same television shows on the Disney Channel and Nickelodeon. So, that means it is acceptable to read the same book or passage over and over. Just like when you are watching a movie for the second time and you see something you didn't recall seeing the first time, when you read something for the second time you understand it better. Have your child get into the practice of reading everything more than once. The magic number is usually three. If the child reads something three times they will be able to read it very well with greater understanding by the third time.

Chapter 17

Technology in Reading

Technology has become the norm these days. Even though paper maps, dictionaries, encyclopedias and yellow pages are still available for use, most people opt to use the electronic format. Children today are accustomed to things as they are now and not how they used to be. For instance, I remember seeing a three-year-old child asking to see the picture after a snapshot was taken of her. She could not understand why she could not see the photograph immediately. The picture had been taken with a disposable camera and that option was not available.

Video games have evolved from the flat black and white version of Pac-Man to Call of Duty Black Ops with a 3-D realistic format. Telephones have changed tremendously as well. We have gone from a cumbersome black rotary phone on a cord that did not have an option of leaving a message or call waiting to the high-tech smart phones of today. Smart phones can do a large array of tasks. They can be used as a camera, video camera, GPS, search engine, and organizer. They are useful for entertainment, such as game playing and watching videos on YouTube.

I have to agree with Marc Pensky, author of Don't Bother Me Mom I'm Learning on encouraging students to use electronic devices for learning. He is of the firm belief that students should have every opportunity to use electronic devices for learning and the teacher and parents should encourage the use of such devices. He refers to the children today as digital natives and those of us born prior to 1980 as digital immigrants.

Children like the speed associated with video games. The colorful scenes and sounds add to the excitement. Why then do we expect a child to be enthusiastic about a white page with black words? There is no excitement there. There is nothing intriguing or the least bit interesting. This is why we should allow children the use of the computer to build their literacy skills. There are free web games such as www.Starfall.com, www.primarygames.com, and www.GrammarGorilla.com . More free resources can be obtained by going to Google and searching for free learning games for children.

Nooks and Kindles are new electronic devices that are replacing paperbound books. Stories can be purchased and downloaded to these devices. The iPad has the same function, with books downloadable from iTunes. They can also be purchased on www.iTunes.com or www.audiobook.com. Both have fees, and you have to purchase the hardcopy of the book yourself in order to read along. Some of the devices are in color and have audio for accompaniment. There is also the old fashioned book on CD. Books on record and on cassette have largely become obsolete, but books are still available on CD. There are a large number of books to choose from and you are not limited to only to the books you can find that come with a CD.

This book is about what we can do to salvage the reading futures of our children who are struggling with the concepts.

Its purpose is to provide parents with hope by providing strategies, resources, and activities to help every child become a confident reader. I have to agree with research that sooner is better than later and the best time to learn to read is at an early age. Learning to read later is like going to the doctor after you are sick, whereas learning to read at an earlier age is like preventive medicine. When you go to the doctor, you will get better, but it is not as good as not getting sick at all.

Early literacy is best. The U.S. Government has programs in place to encourage early literacy. This includes learning to read in kindergarten through third grade and being a competent reader by the end of third grade. Many things can be done to support this. Expose your child to literacy concepts before they start school. Sing the alphabet song repeatedly in the car. Make watching Sesame Street a requirement before any other show can be viewed. Play rhyming games like "I'm thinking of a word that rhymes with cat, you wear it on your head so it must be a... hat." Read to your child often. Daily reading is best.

The new reading sensation, *Your Baby Can Read* is not new at all. I used the program 37 years ago when my daughter was three years old. Of course the program was not as advanced as it is today. There was no electronic component of the programs. Some of the cards came preprinted and the others had to be written out by the parent. The program was very effective then as it is now. It is taught to very young children with memorization and repetition. If all children could have the opportunity to experience this program at a young age, it would greatly decrease the number of older children not reading on grade level. I have heard many people complain that the child is not really reading, does not understand what they read, or cannot decode unknown words. Even if this is true of two- or three-year-old, it gives them something to build on and they will understand and decode once they are developmentally ready. It is better the have something to build on that not to have any exposure to written texts at an early age.

Some children get their first exposure to academics once they enter the kindergarten classroom. Like the well known book by Masaru Ibuka states, *Kindergarten is Too Late.* Children not reading upon entry to kindergarten often have difficulty learning due to the large class sizes and lack of individualized attention. Any opportunity a child has to learn at an early age should be supported and encouraged. It is easier and less frustrating for the child when they can learn without the pressure of expectation in the classroom.

Chapter 18

Activities and Strategies that Work

Long before the movie *The Color Purple* came out, in which Celie learned to read from her sister Nettie, I have used the reading activity of labeling everything in the house so that my young children could become familiar with and recognize the written words of everyday objects. I would label everything in sight: table, chair, light switch, bookshelf, curtain, even the trash can. This is an effective method of exposing nonreaders to the printed word.

Chapter 19

Sample Study

I conducted a sample study with five sixth grade students who were reading far below grade level. I had signed parent consents to include the students in the study, as well as signed approval from the school district to conduct the study. Additionally, the teachers of the students were very supportive. Part of the reason for the success of the study was the small group size. There were several components of the program used in the study.

Progress Monitoring

Frequent progress monitoring was a key element in this program. It allowed the researcher to determine which concepts had been mastered, which were improving and which needed more instructions. Students worked on deficit concepts during their daily center time, and progress monitoring occurred on a continuous basis; however, only weekly progress was charted as documentation for the application project. Parents and guardians were provided with weekly progress reports which went home on Friday. They were encouraged to respond and given the opportunity to discuss any concerns via telephone with the researcher.

OTHER IMPORTANT ELEMENTS

Putting It All Together includes other research-based components that have proven effective in student achievement. Music is used to raise morale and also to teach some specific concepts. Some students learn better and can comprehend and retain information when it is presented to them in a musical format. **Howard Gardner's Theory of Multiple Intelligences** identifies that there are many forms of intelligence and that people have varying strengths and combinations of these. Musical Rhythmic Intelligence, ("music smart"), is the capacity to think musically. It means that a student is able to hear patterns, recognize them, and perhaps manipulate them. People who have strong musical intelligence do not just remember music easily, they can not get it out of their minds.

Care is implemented throughout the program. Students should be made aware of the teacher's concern for their learning. Nel Noddings' research reports that care is an important element in education. She explained that students are more susceptible to achievement when they sense their teacher cares about them and their progress. Motivation is also important to the success of this program. Students need to be motivated in order to achieve ultimate success. Many of the students have developed learned helplessness. They are viewed as lazy or unmotivated by their classroom teacher. They are so lost and overwhelmed with their expectations that it is easier to do nothing, because the frustration they experience when trying to do the work is too great to endure. In an effort to improve student motivation, incentives are used, because the researcher wants full student participation without reluctance. Students are more likely to do their best and achieve their highest potential when they are willingly participating and putting forth their best effort.

Parent participation was also a required feature in the program. According to a review of recent research published by the Southwest Educational Development Laboratory (2002), students whose parents were involved, no matter what their income or background, were more likely to earn higher grades and test scores, enroll in higher-level programs, be promoted, pass their classes, earn credits, attend school regularly, have better social skills, show improved behavior, adapt well to school, graduate, and go on to post-secondary education. Furthermore, studies show that families of all income and education levels, and from all ethnic and cultural groups, are engaged in supporting their children's learning at home. White, middle-class families, however, tend to be more involved at school, and to be better informed about how to help their children. Parent involvement at school from all families may be an important strategy for addressing the achievement gap.

CONCLUSIONS AND FINDINGS

The researcher attempted to make this program include all the major key elements of promoting student success. The mindset was, "If all these things were proven to be successful, why not combine them and obtain optimum success?" The results were positive; however, a major hindrance in the application of the program was that it worked best with small groups of five students or less. If the program could be developed to support more students, there could be a significant improvement in student achievement that will positively close the achievement gap.

Five students were monitored for the purpose of this book. There were fifteen students participating in the study. The first order of business was to obtain permission from the district to use the students in my project as part of my work for Walden University. I submitted a copy of my letter for parent authorization along with the letter of request to the director of pupil services. I have a letter on school district letterhead granting me approval for the study. A copy of the letter is included in the Appendix. The letters were sent home with fifteen students and the first five to be returned were included in the study.

Surveys for parents and students were taken to obtain information about student reading habits and history. These were useful in determining commonalities in the students with reading deficits. A copy of the letter is included in the Appendix.

Each student was given three timed tests to determine a base reading level. The chart below explains the results.

Student Name	Date of Base 9/18	10/2	10/16	10/30	11/13	11/27	12/11
HM61101	60, 46, 57	97	93	99	101	103	104
BM61202	85, 78, 79	106	130	108	112	119	126
HM61103	35, 45*, 51*	43	56	47	51	59	65
HF61304	74, 66, 71	99	105	141	118	123	135
BM61105	91, 82, 93	116	122	131	140	145	150

The scores above reflect the students' initial reading score when reading a grade

An asterisk indicates a below-grade level passage. Each student read three different passages which were timed for one minute. The median score of the three was used. _ indicates median score.

Instructions were given to the students two times a week. They used the R.E.W.A.R.D.S. program and also a modified version of Read Naturally. After two weeks of instructions, the student were tested again using an unfamiliar grade level reading passage. All students had an increase in words read per minute. The increase of words read per minute varied from 8 to 40 words per minute.

Student HM61101 had three timed readings to determine his base reading score. The medium score of 57 was used. His other two scores were 46 and 60. This student tried hard to improve his reading. Each week he made improvement. There was a 40-word gain after the first two weeks of instructions. The following two weeks showed a decrease of four words. There were two weeks of instruction between each timed session. The following two weeks yielded a five-word growth. After this point, growth remained constant and steady, with weekly growth.

See the corresponding graph on next page

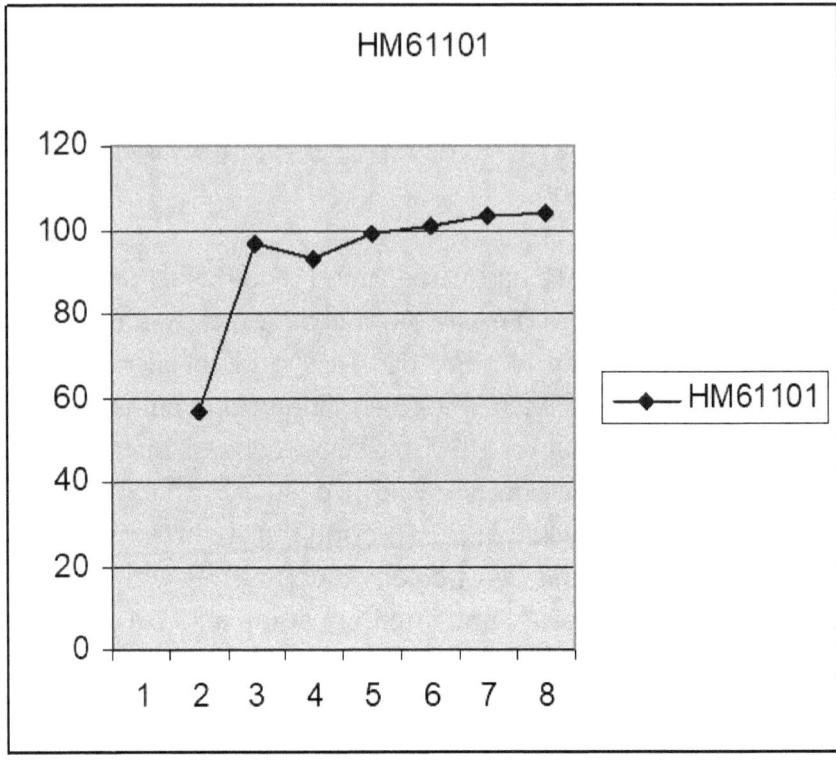

Student BM611202's scores were much higher than the previous student's. His median score was 79, with the other two scores being 78 and 85. This student read at a fast pace without regard to punctuation. He mowed over words he did not know and miscalled the words. He was not careful that what he read made sense. After the first two weeks of instruction, his reading improved by 25 words per minute. His next measurement yielded another 24-word growth. This growth was maintained and determined when the student had a really good day. The next reading was 108, just two words more than his original 25 word gain, but 22 words less than his last read. His next three readings showed growth. His words per minute were, 112, 119, and 126. Overall his word gain was 47 words in the 12-week period.

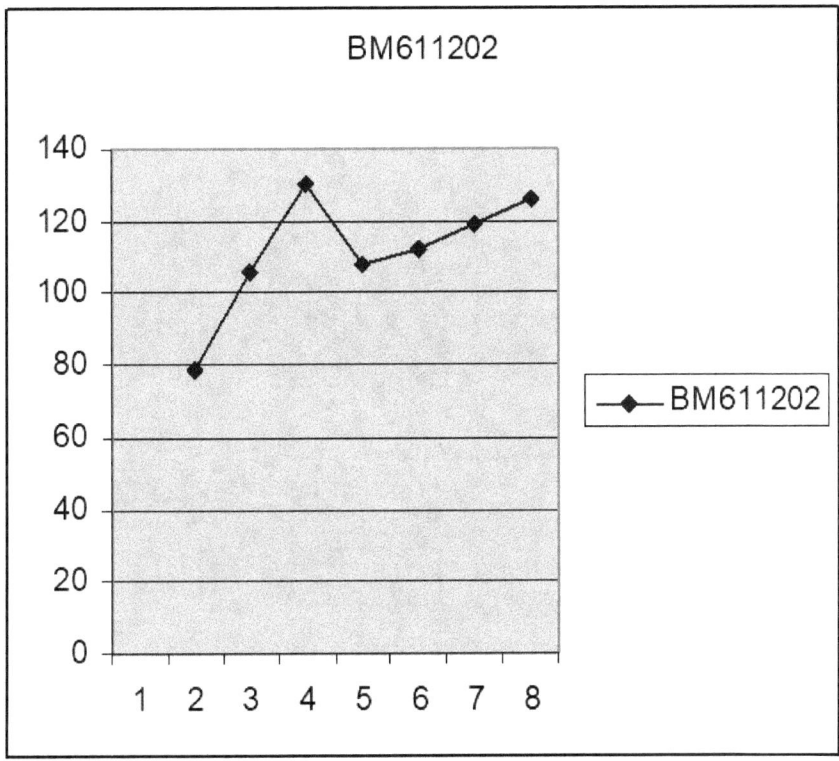

Student HM61103 struggled when reading the grade level passage. He was allowed to read a fifth grade passage for his second two readings. The grade level score was used as a base. The lower passages were used to prevent undue frustration for the student, as it was clear that he struggled. His assessment after two weeks of instruction was a grade level passage. He made an 8-word increase. The following two weeks showed a 13-word increase. He had a decrease the following session. The last six weeks his gain was as follows: 51, 59, and 65. His final read was 30 words more per minute, almost 100% growth over the 35 words per minute he read originally.

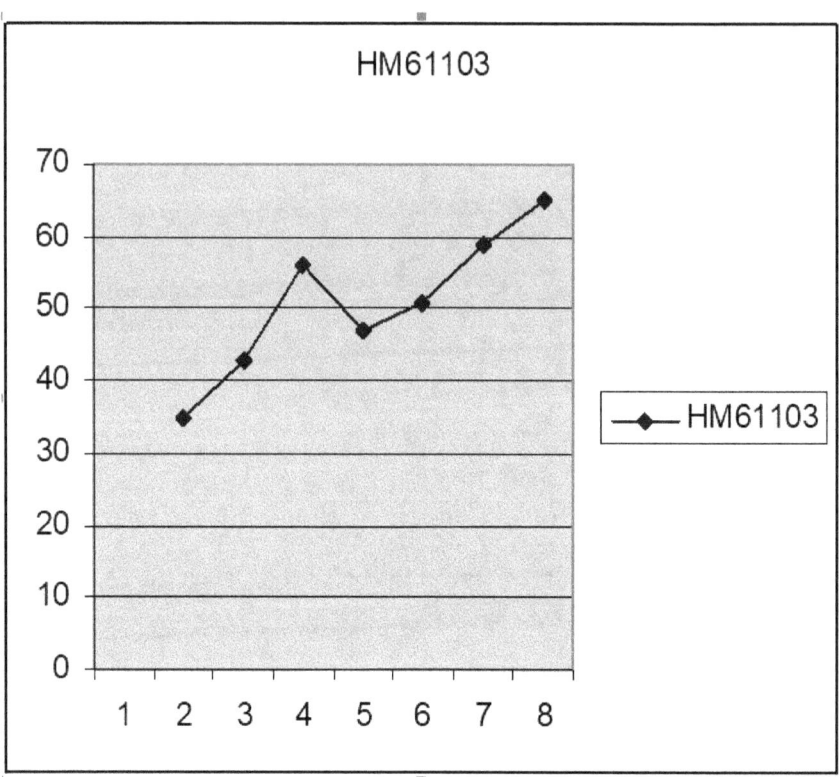

Student HF61304 was the only female included in the study. She was older than the other students and of Hispanic descent. She was pressured by her parents to improve her reading. They told her she would repeat sixth grade if her reading does not improve. This is not an option the school would exercise, as she already repeated a grade in the past. Her base median score was 71. The first reading after two weeks was 99, an 18-word gain.

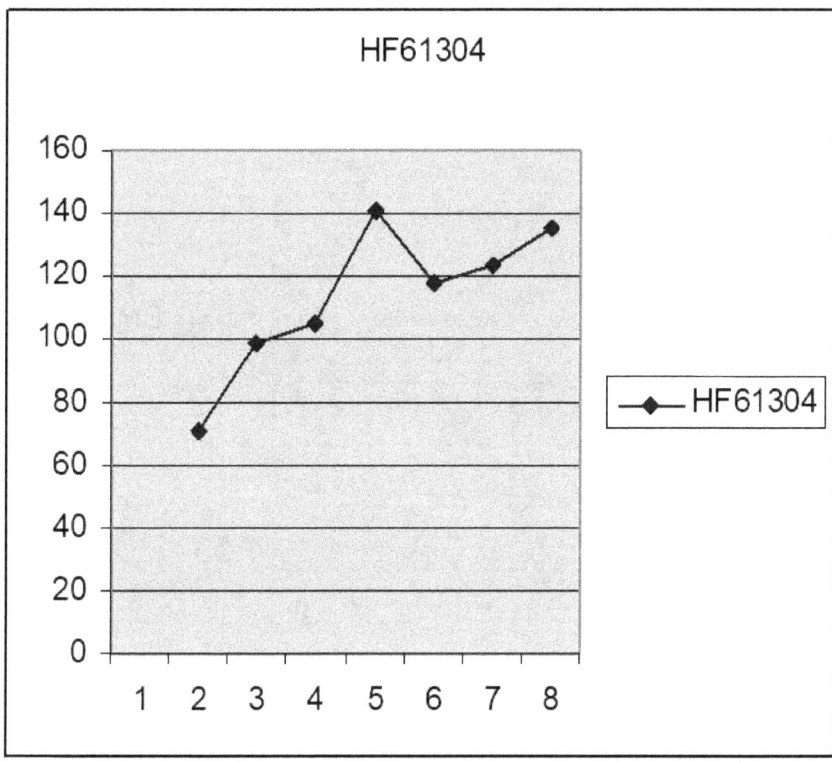

Student BM61105 had the highest initial score. Apparently, he read better for me than for his teacher because he recommended him for the reading program I was teaching. He was more confident in the small setting with other students that he knew had reading difficulties than in the regular classroom. His base score was 91. His high was 93 and the low 85. After the first two weeks of intense instruction, he scored 116, a 24-word gain. He had a slight decrease in the following read with only 112 wpm. The next four measurements were as follows: 131, 140, 145, 150.

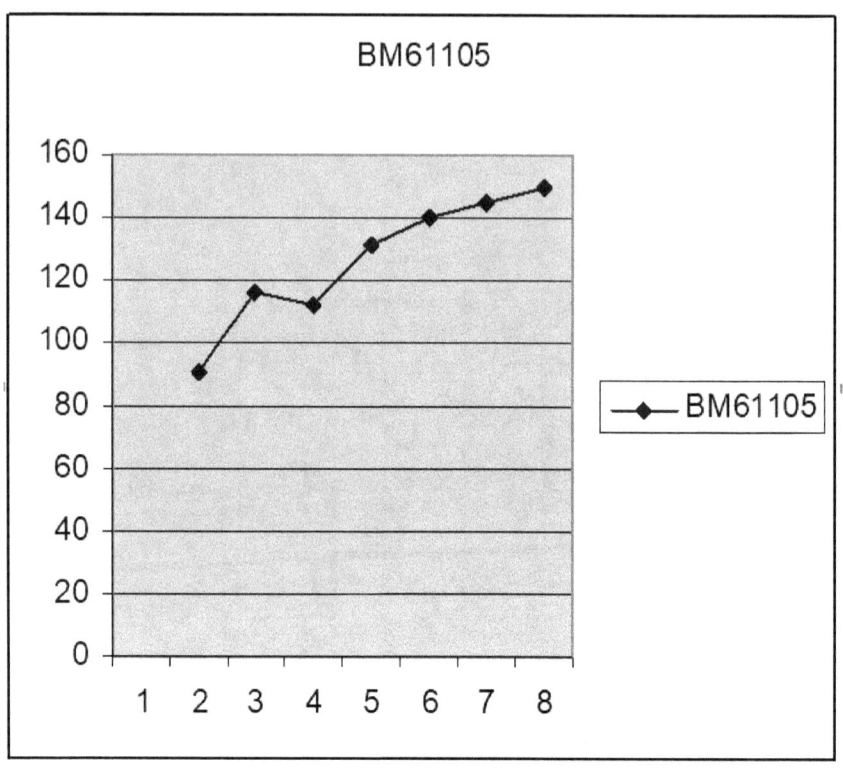

It can be seen that all students made growth during the 12-week period of the
program. The two weeks between the each measurement were filled with intense direct
instruction. The instruction varied from week to week. In the course of the instruction, a quick overview of the LiPS program with emphasis on mastering the vowel circle was given. Each section was learned separately. First, the Smiles were learned: ee, i, e, ae, a, and u. They were taught for only one day, but reviewed daily for three weeks. Next, the Opens— o, au, and aw—and the Rounds—oe, oo, and ōō—were taught for one day and reviewed daily thereafter for three weeks. On the third day the Sliders were taught—ue, ie, ou, ow, oi, and

oy—for one day and reviewed daily, as the others were. On the fourth day the Bully Rs, er,ir,ur,ar and or, were taught.

During the first week each day started with the LiPs Lesson. It was followed by timed readings of grade level passages. They students read the passage three times while being timed. First the students were asked to read an unfamiliar passage to themselves for one minute. They were asked to highlight the last word they read with a green highlighter. Then the instructor asked the students to read the passage in its entirety, circling the words they either did not recognize or did that they did not comprehend with a red pen. The instructor then read the passage to the students, addressing all unknown words and their definitions. The instructor used examples, stories and scenarios to make the definition clear to the students in a way they could relate to. After the unknown words and vocabulary had been addressed, the students did two more timed readings. Generally there was a large gain once the students were familiar with the vocabulary, and growth was made with each student reading on a daily basis. The student underlined the second read with a blue pen and highlighted the third read with a yellow highlighter. The color-coded method assisted the teacher in seeing the progress at a glance. Once the vowel circle from the LiPs program was mastered, the students were taught using the R.E.W.A.R.D.S. program. This program focused on multi-syllable words. Affixes were learned in isolation and students learned to locate the root word and break down a word for quick decoding. This program is usually used for students reading above 2.3 grade level, and there are a total of only twenty lessons in the program. Students were only taught the first ten lessons.

The next program used was the Vocabulary program. It came with colored photo cards, flashcards, student workbooks and a teacher manual. Each lesson taught seven new vocabulary words. The photo cards were shown to the students as a sentence was read describing the picture. The flashcards were displayed in the front of the classroom at the white board so the word could be associated with the picture. The instructor then read a story to the students using the vocabulary. Then the students had to complete three pages of vocabulary-related work in the workbook. Each day we reviewed the word learned on the previous days. Students received points for using any newly taught vocabulary word in their conversations. The students also read timed passages three times to increase their fluency. This activity was also led by the teacher. When the teacher did individual timed reading, the students completed various activities related to the passage.

Chapter 20

Reading is Developmental

Research supports the theory and I will be the first to agree that reading is developmental. I have mentioned before that I am the natural (biological) mother of eleven children. I have come to know that reading, much like walking and talking, is. The average age at which a baby walks is one year old. Many babies walk by ten months old, some babies walk as early as seven months and others walk as late as sixteen months. No matter at what age a baby begins walking, it does not mean they will not walk as well as a child who walked at an earlier age. When the children are all five years old and running around on the kindergarten playground, no one can look at any one of the children and determine at which age he/she first walked. Once the skill of walking is mastered over a period of time, one child walks as well as the next, even if they did not learn at the same age. Just like walking, reading is developmental. All children do not read at the same age and can not be expected to achieve the skill by a certain age. Just like some babies walk long after a year, some children will master reading long after third grade. Once the child has learned to read and becomes a fluent competent reader, he/she will be able to read as well as any other child his age, even those who learned to read at an earlier age.

If a child is not walking by the age of three, no one says the child is a lost cause and will never walk. Instead steps are taken to make sure the child has a support in learning to walk. Physical exams and other testing will be given to the child. Support such as physical therapy will be provided if needed. Crutches or a walker will be provided if needed. There is no way anyone will allow a child to just sit without any support when learning to walk, even if it means they do so with assistance. Likewise, students not reading independently on their own should be supported with the same concern and enthusiasm as a child not walking by a certain age is supported and encouraged.

Chapter 21

Common Core

In the first edition of this book I mentioned that reading instruction should continue until students are able to read proficiently and not cease at the end of third grade. I honestly feel that reading support should continue until reading has been mastered. When Common Core was introduced it included the foundational skill to fifth grade which was extended. Prior to this, foundational skills were only taught to third grade. Foundational skills are the skills a student has to master completely before they can become fluent readers. Foundational skills include: the concept of print, alphabets and sounds, phonemic awareness, phonics, sight words and fluency.

There has been research done (which I did not agree with) that if a student could not read by the end of 3rd grade they would never catch up and that jail cell were planned for these students, year before they reach adulthood. All of nothing is ever anything. All babies do not have teeth at six months old. All babies do not walk by their first birthday. All children do not read by the end of third grade, but with continued reading support and being proactive they will read and read as well as anyone else. Reading is developmental. Every child does not master it at the same age, but with continued support all children can become proficient readers.

What else is different about Common Core reading? Close reading is one of the concepts emphasized by Common Core. Close reading in the process of doing a deep read of the text and evaluating every line of the content. It is studying what each word means and why it is included in the text. It includes repeated readings of the same text with discussions and analysis to gain a better understanding. Close reading looks at the author's reason for choosing which words are used in the passage and how the words are related to the overall meaning of the passage.

Chapter 22

Reading and Distance Learning

Teaching reading through distance learning was a challenge. It was unexpected and unplanned, but once student and teachers across America were forced to implement distance learning, it was imperative that reading instructions were given in that manner. One way that reading was done was in a small group setting. Teachers would have three to five student at a time and they would take turns reading as though they were live and in person. Each student would read when called upon by the teacher. With guided reading the teacher would correct the student when they made and error and provided tips to assist the student in sounding out words or using in text content or pictures to help with the unknown word.

There were also many on-line reading programs that were offered (many times for free) to assist student with reading. Readlive which is the computer version of Read Naturally was reformatted to allow the parent to have access to read with their student. Jack Hartman has many videos of various levels of sight words. The Letter Factory sounds out the alphabets with objects to represent each sound. There were many other videos that provided the same concepts.

Audio books were also used for the classic classroom chapter books. The teacher would play the audio book as the student followed along with the PDF on the screen. This was done instead of having a book delivered to each students' home or having the students pick the books up from the school during the classroom work distribution times. This was effective and allowed the students access without the added burden of lost, damaged or never returned books. The PDF copy as well as each copy of the audio book were posted on the Google Classroom which allowed the students the ability to re-read and or re listen to any chapter that they missed, didn't fully understand, or wanted to hear or read again.

Parents were able to access the resources and share the reading experience along with their child. They could discuss, and question the student about the events in the book, by asking the child about their thoughts, discussing vocabulary words and comparing the events to real life situations. Some parents opted to order a hard copy from Amazon, so that the student could read along with their own book and keep it to add to their personal library.

Chapter 23

Ortin Gillingham

Ortin Gillingham is a multi-sensory reading program. Student get to use movement and gestures as well as texture to assist them in learning and remembering the letter sounds, syllabication, spelling, and letter formation. Ortin Gillingham (OG) instruction can only be provided by trained professional who have had the training directly from the company and are skilled in knowing how to provide the instruction correctly. If you are looking for a reading tutor for your child ask if the tutor is trained in Ortin Gillingham. The strategies are very effective and the reading improvement that your child makes will be immediate and obvious.

I took the training myself in 2019, a year before the Pandemic. The summer of 2019 I taught my five year old granddaughter to read using OG. She was refusing to go to kindergarten unless she could read. We tried without success to explain to her that she did not need to know how to read to a go to kindergarten. She could not and would not understand that. I agreed to teach her to read during the summer break. That way I could practice using the OG strategies that I had just learned. I worked with her two times a week for seven weeks. She already knew the alphabet and sounds (which was very helpful). The first sound I had to teach her was qu. We then learned, the digraphs, ch, sh, wh, th and ph. Then we learned the sending double sounds, ll, ss, ff and dd. After that she took off on her own and just started reading everything. She was reading billboards and signs riding down the street in the car. One day I heard her reading closed captions from the television. I knew at that moment that she was actually an independent reader. She started kindergarten only to realize that none of the other students could read and most of them were still learning their alphabets and sounds. She decided that should would not let the teacher know she could read, so that she could be like the other students. The teacher soon discovered her ability to read and notified her Mom. "I don't think you know this, but your daughter can read".

During the same time, I taught a second grade boy to read through my tutoring company. I worked with him two times a week for sixteen weeks. I used his word list from his teacher as the red words that we practiced writing in the sand, writing on the grid with a red crayon, taping out and spelling. The little boy absolutely loved games, so we played, memory match where he had to find the same word twice and read it out loud, Bam where he had to read the words to get points, teacher made board games and card games using the words. We read stories that had the words in them. We also write words and sentences. The strategies proved effective. I asked about his reading six month later and was told, "he knows how to read, he is just lazy and doesn't really want to read".

Chapter 24

Strategies and Activities

(Helps to strengthen the reading skills of struggling students)

- Talk to your child about the importance of reading.
- Watch the movie *Bluffing It* with Dennis Weaver.
- Watch familiar shows with closed-captions (no sound).
- Read together and discuss the story.
- Read to your child.
- Have your child read to you.
- Read out loud at the same time. (coral reading).
- Practice using synonym for everyday things.
- Label household items.
- Write notes to your child.
- Read a book, then watch the movie with the same title.
- Compare the movie and book.
- Text or instant message your child.
- Email your child.
- Allow your child to read you the mail.
- Have the child read the recipe while you cook.

- Have the child read directions when you drive.
- Get books and magazine of interest to your child.
- Have child read the book while listening to audio book.
- Allow reading on electronic devices.
- Set aside a family reading time.
- Provide incentive at home for improved reading grade.
- Have book available everywhere (car, backpack).
- Encourage 90 total minutes of reading a daily.
- Read in small groups (5 students or less).
- Make flash cards (play games with flashcards).
- Games: BINGO, BAM, Memory Match, Fast Read
- Read the billboards and street signs out loud in car,

About the Author

Dr. Sarah ShaBazz has a PhD in Education with emphasis in Special Education. Sarah is a professional educator and has teaching credentials in both general and special education. She has experience teaching students from kindergarten through Master's degree university level. Sarah is the founder of a mobile tutoring company that provides educational support to students of all ages. She is a revered civic leader and is on the board of several organizations that supports women, their families, and the community. She is the biological mother of 11 children: six sons and five daughters. Sarah is the author of five books and also publishes books for other authors.

Cover Artist: Camila Câmara (Instagram name: smillallart)

More Books by Dr. ShaBazz

Other products:

- So Many Books (Rhyming book)
- Two Grand (Compare and Contrast)
- Modern Medicine (Compare and Contrast)
- The Name Game (Finding Value in a Name)
- So Many More Books (Part 2, rhyming book)
- A Parent's Guide to Making Every Child a Reader

Coming Soon

- A Teacher's Guide to Making Every Child a Reader
- Books Are Fun for Everyone – Musical CD
- Books Are Fun for Everyone – Educator Pack
- The Name Game